A Book of Thoughts;

Longing for Heaven

Vol. 1

Angela Tibbs

A Book of Thoughts;

Longing For Heaven Vol. 1& 2

Bell Sheep Publishing

2i4 E. 10th St

Georgetown, Illinois   61846

bellpublishing17@gmail.com

(217)474-0410

© 2013, 2025, Bell Sheep Publishing

ISBNS;

Paperback; 979-8-9906561-6-1

Ebook;   979-8-9906561-7-8

Dedicated To:

To all the family, friends, and strangers who helped inspire these poems. That will help others as they find their way to heaven while on their journey on earth.

Table Of Contents

Perfect

I tried to be perfect in everyone's eyes
Inside I was torn apart
Great expectations were too much for me
I always seem to disappoint the people who love me

Being perfect is what one person can't be
Who's perfect, who's perfect, who's perfect
No one person can be
Perfect, perfect, perfect, perfect

For years I've tried to live up to the friends I chose
It had been a burden for me
Until the day I learned
The only person I had to please was myself

Being perfect is what one person can't be
Who's perfect, who's perfect, who's perfect
No one person can be
Perfect, perfect, perfect, perfect

Positive State of Mind

In the mornin, I'm lyin there in bed
The devil puts negative thoughts in my head
Off the beatin path I was lead
By the angel that's spiritually dead
But on the word of God I fed
To start my day in a positive way

There are days my troubles aren't few
That's why Jesus I turned to you
When it seems I'm in a bind
I quote the scripture line for line
Cause I'm determined to stay
In a positive state of mind

When the mountains are tall
My back's up against the wall
To the world it's no secret at all
The devil wants me to stumble and fall
Tellin me the Bible's words are null
So I can't hear the Lord's call

There are days my troubles aren't few
That's why Jesus I turn to you
When is seems I'm in a bind
I quote the scripture line for line
Cause I'm determined to stay
In a positive state of mind

Tomorrow's Another Day

You could have heard a pin drop
When my aunt told us the news
Informin us she had cancer
We all started to think oh, what will she do
Then we remembered what Grandpa Bill would say

If you take the bad
There's bound to be some good
Make sure to live everyday
Cause tomorrow's another day

4

Lately, we've thought about him a lot
Back when he was dying with cancer
Facin it head on knowin the outcome
He lived every day to the fullest
And he would always say

If you take the bad
There's bound to be some good
Make sure to live everyday
Cause tomorrow's another day

A Gift

Time runs at a fast pace
How quickly the hours pass
Money makes the world go around
Simpler times have slipped away
We barely take time for ourselves
People in need our forgotten
The elderly are abused
All we need to be is a gift

You're a gift
When you share a smile
You're a gift
When you sit and talk awhile
You're a gift
When goin that extra mile
Sharin God's love with someone

It's simple just give a little time

Workin in a nursing home
The atmosphere is sad and blue
There are patients who have no family at all
While for others, there family don't care
Some days I hate to go to work
Cause I just want to cry
Society has seemed to throw them away
When they can still share the gift of love

I'm goin to be a gift
When I share a smile
I'm goin to be a gift
When I sit and talk awhile
I'm goin to be a gift
As I go that extra mile
Sharin God's love with someone
And simply just give a little time

Stumblin to Heaven

I'm stumblin to heaven
Yes, I'm stumblin to heaven
Through every trial and tribulation
(Walking through every storm)
Slowly stumblin my way closer to the joys of heaven
But I'm stumblin (oh, yes)
I'm stumblin to heaven

Born in the shadow of someone else
I worked to make a success of myself
Not wantin to put my life on a shelf
Unsurely made it through the hand I was dealt
Movin forward in spite of everyone else
Slowly findin strength within myself

Believin each step was the right one
I wouldn't listen to anyone
Knowin that it seemed to everyone
I'd lost my chance to start over again
Didn't expect to hear the Lord say "Well done"
Even if it was a gospel song I sung

It's never easy to come to a crossroad
Choosin to live the way I was told
Or believin the devil would carry my heavy load

I'm stumblin to heaven
Yes, I'm stumblin to heaven
Through every trial and tribulation
(Walkin through every storm)
Slowly stumblin my way closer to the joys of heaven
But, I'm stumblin to heaven (oh, yes)
I'm stumblin to heaven

Last Stop Before Heaven

We're born into this world
Quickly we grow to from child to adult
Days are spent workin for the dollar
Our children grow as fast as weeds
Before we know it, we're the older generation
Thought to be fragile enough to break
Our family believes that best place for us
Is a nursin home where we feel useless

It's the last stop before heaven
A chance to reminisce with new friends
Bein a teacher to the younger generation
Tellin about simpler times
When everything revolved around family
Instead of keepin up with the world
It's the last stop before heaven
Until I'm ready to be with my Lord

I find myself reachin out to God
Gettin back on the straight and narrow
After spendin many years astray
It's nice to have people who listen
To my ramblin stories of the past
They don't know how much it means
Seein a smile or listenin ear
When I sometimes feel alone

My life trials are almost over
But yet there is so much I can do

It's the last stop before heaven
A chance to reminisce with new friends
Bein a teacher to the younger generation
Tellin about simpler times
When everything revolved around family
Instead of keepin up with the world
It's the last stop before heaven
Until I'm ready to be with my Lord

A Second Chance

I was raised on the Good Book
Went to church every Sunday
Put on the path to the Promise Land
In an ever changin world that gettin crazier

With values of yesterday slippin away
I listened to every word that preacher did say
Learnin Jesus was comin back someday
Knowin that day of judgment I can't delay

To be embraced back into his arms
Cleansed by the blood of Jesus
My many unforgiveable sins washed away
Gettin a second chance to start over again

Now, I'm livin on my own
Bombarded by the devil's temptations
Willingly walkin into darkness
My faith in Jesus was no more

I'd convinced myself my life had just begun
Intentionally, I turned my back on God's only son
Until I was standin alone with a loaded gun

As I stood there tryin to decide to whether to live or die
The Lord reached out his hand and said "I will never lie"

To be embraced back into his arms
Cleansed by the blood of Jesus
My many unforgiveable sins washed away
Gettin a second chance to start over again

The Neighborhood Church

He was born in East Tupelo
Attended the local Pentecostal Church
Spent many afternoons singin on the porch
At twelve he received a guitar
Taught how to play by family and friends
He told everyone of his opry dreams
Determined to take care of his mama
He believed a brighter future was to come

The neighborhood church
Was where he learned God's word
The neighborhood church
Was where he found Jesus
The neighborhood church
Was where he learned how to sing
The neighborhood church
Was where he heard the Lord's call

Wantin a chance to start over
Vernon moved them up to Memphis. Tennessee

Elvis attended all night gospel singins
Takin in the meltin pot of music
His own style begun to emerge
Determined to become the biggest star in the world
He went into Sun Studio made a record
Hopin his life would soon change

Elvis Presley's life become a roller coaster ride
As he daily dealt with fame and fortune
Turnin to the Bible for guidance
Sharin his love of gospel music with fans
Bringin it to the mainstream society
Givin people hope in their darkest hour
In Elvis' quest to leave a legacy of love
He brought many people to the Lord

The neighborhood church
Was where he learned God's word
The neighborhood church
Was where he found Jesus
The neighborhood church
Was where he learned how to sing
The neighborhood church
Was where he heard the Lord's call

Its Heyday is Gone

Many stories have I been told
A little church on an Arkansas red dirt road
People findin their love for singin
Cuttin their teeth on Amazin Grace
Preacher preachin about hell and temptation
Children sittin on the edge of their seats
The Bible bein taught with such emotion
Grown-ups loudly shoutin Amen

The church's heyday is gone
For a congregation it longs
To hear an upliftin spiritual song
Goin back to a much simpler time
When people helped each other on a dime
Especially, if someone was in a bind
But, the church's heyday is gone
Yes, its heyday is gone

Times have changed yet there still the same
God and family are the most important
The church was long ago abandoned
Still everyone is welcome inside
Lit by the light though a broken windo
A faded picture of Jesus hangs on the wall
Under layer of thick cobwebs and dust
On the pulpit lays a worn out Bible

The church's heyday is gone
For a congregation it longs
To hear an upliftin spiritual song
Goin back to a much simpler time
When people would help each other on a dime
Especially, if someone was in a bind
But, the church's heyday is gone
Yes, its heyday is gone

Many souls were saved in that little church
They've in turn help spread the gospel word

The church's heyday is gone
For a congregation it longs
Yes, its heyday is gone

Plan B

Plan A was to give my life to Jesus
Livin each day by his word
Takin time to study the Bible
So I can to know the Lord
But livin in this busy old world
There're not enough minutes in the day
To spend some quiet time with him
So like many others, I began to

Live my life by plan B
Fallin short of my promises
Givin into the devil's temptations
Cause I'm tired of fightin the spiritual fight
I go to church every Sunday to be taught his word
Then I go back into this sinful world
Tryin to live my life by plan A
But somehow settle for plan B

Plan A was to help people in trouble
Sharin the Lord's gospel word
Showin he really does love them

Especially, if they've lost their way
Cause everyone gets a second chance
To get their life back on the right path
That leads up to the pearly gates
When it comes to myself to my dismay, I still

Live my life by plan B
Fallin short of my promises
Givin into the devil's temptations
Cause I'm tired of fightin the spiritual fight
I go to church every Sunday to be taught his word
Then I go back into this sinful world
Tryin to live my life by plan A
But somehow settle for plan B

Plan A was to rededicate my life to Jesus
To get my life back on the right road
Stop comin up with silly excuses
Makin the best of another chance
Take time to read the Good Book
To know my Lord and savior
Helpin other people along the way
And live by his word, but still I

Live my life by plan B

I'll Meet You at the Gate

(Dedicated to Virgil Scott)

On the day you decided to leave
I was filled with sadness and anger
Wonderin how I would make it without you
Both my eyes filled with tears
Knownin I've lost my best friend
As family and friends sit around
I think of the many good times we've shared
And can't wait until the day

I'll meet you at the gate
When it's my time to meet the Lord
I'll meet you at the gate
When my vacation on earth is done
I'll meet you at the gate
As you patiently wait for me
I'll meet you at the gate
When I come home to heaven

Life will never be the same
Since I can't see your smile
Hear that contagious laugh
Or see the sparkle in your eyes
Knownin you're watchin from above
Helps me get out of bed each day
Readin the Bible I find faith
But, I can't wait until the day

I'll meet you at the gate
When it's my time to meet the Lord
I'll meet you at the gate
When my vacation on earth is done
I'll meet you at the gate
As you wait patiently for me
I'll meet you at the gate
When I come home to heaven

It's Not About You

The world's gettin crazier everyday
We all want are fifteen minutes of fame
Takin credit for the glory
When it's not ours to have
Steppin away from material things
We learn what's so important
Fellowshippin with each other
And givin praise to the one above

It's not about you
It's not about me
It's about helpin each other
We're all wantin to believe
There are people who care
Tryin to spread the word
That someone cares so much
He gave his begotten son

Life on earth is short
We have to enjoy livin each day
Thinkin less of I and more of others
Findin time to read the Good Book
Figurin out the directions to heaven
Learnin there's trouble in our path
We need the help of others
To get us where we're bound

It's not about you
It's not about me
It's about the helpin each other
We're all wantin to believe
There are people who care
Tryin to spread the word
That someone cares so much
He gave his only begotten son

Jesus is in the Boat

The thunder is rollin
The wind is blowin
The lightin is crackin
Sittin in this little boat I wondered
Will I make it through this storm
The rain began to pour down
As the boat tossed and turned
Lowerin my head to pray
Lord, help me and then I remembered

Jesus is in the boat
When the winds begin to blow
Jesus is in the boat
When the storm is strong
Jesus is in the boat
All I have to do is believe
Realizin he's watchin over me
Waitin for me to call on him

Life on earth isn't easy
The wind can sometimes be breezy
Believin in God's word
Havin just a little faith
I'm not goin through any storm alone
He's right beside me
Because I remembered

Jesus is in the boat
When the winds begin to blow
Jesus is in the boat
When the storm is strong
Jesus is in the boat
All I have to do is believe
Realizin he's watchin over me
Waitin for me to call on him

Home To Heaven

(Dedicated to Betty Ruble)

When Betty left us so unexpectedly
Weeks later many were still in shock
Our eyes filled with tears
The sunrise we selfishly tried to block

But havin faith calmed our fears
We heard every minute of the ticking clock
She had made many friends though out the years
Cause her light had always shined bright

She's gone home to heaven
To reunite with those who have gone before
Spreadin her wings to soar
Her vacation on earth was over

Her life seemed to be so brief

Much more could she have done
For many it was too hard to believe
Never passed up the chance to have fun
No familiar friend would she deceive
Livin like she was twenty years young
Always the last one to leave
This little light was the song she always sung

She's gone home to heaven
To reunite with those who have gone before
Spreadin her wings to soar
Her vacation days on earth are over
It was never meant for her to stay
She waited until everyone would be ok
Betty then went home to heaven
Oh, yes, she went home to heaven

The void left inside will be hard to fill
She'll remain in our hearts until we meet again
Betty went home to heaven
Oh, yes, she's went home to heaven

LOVE

You say you love me
That word comes easy for you
Lettin me know how you care
Wantin me to fall in love too
Makin me the light of your world
Every minute away is chillin
You want me to be by your side
Shownin me exactly how you feel

Love, it's a strong word
So heavy that it scares me
Of puttin my heart on the line
Only to get my heart broken
I hide it away from anyone
Who gets so close enough to touch
Cause love is so life changin
Cause I can't say it until I'm ready

Content to live my life alone
I wasn't lookin for love
Knownin how easily it can fall apart
Then you stepped into my life

Lettin me see how I could be loved
Resistin not wantin to risk my heart
I was afraid to say that four letter word
That means so much and is so precious

Believin this is a partnership
No important decision is made alone
Bein honest with one another
My heart will open up
Without bein afraid, I can say I love you
Not scared of that small word
Puttin my heart on the line
Willin to take a chance

Love, it's a strong word
So heavy that it scares me
Of puttin my heart on the line
Only to get it broken
I hide it from anyone
Who gets close enough to touch
Cause love is so life changin
I can't say it until I'm ready

Lost & Found

Born into this world
I grew up getting everything
Believin I did nothin wrong
Alcohol was my best friend
Partyin was my life
I was walkin the road to hell

I was lost in darkness
I was lost in sin
Lost in the world systems
Deceived by the devil's lies
I was goin in circles
Endin up at the same destination

Then someone reached out
Showin me how I'd been deceived

Tellin me there was a man
Who would wash my sins away
All I have to do is believe
And give my life to him

I found a second chance
I found salvation
Seeing the glorious light
Findin the Lord truly loves me
I read his word daily
I'm now walkin the road to heaven

We all have a choice to make
It's up to us just where our destination ends

I was lost until I found the light
I was lost until I found salvation
I was lost until I found his word
I was once on the road to hell
Now, I'm walkin toward heaven

Dark Times

Darkness seems to sneak up, when things are goin great
Tryin to break my faith, taken a cheap shot at me
Usin words of much untruth to put doubt in my soul
Believin he's won the devil dances
He's dumbfounded as I reach for my Bible

Dark times don't last strong faithful people do
The world wants my light dimmed
But it gets brighter each day
Dark times don't last the word of God is forever
Believin the promises he made
Those dark times will just disappear

Sometimes people can be mean
As they believe the devil's lies
Whisperin that Jesus doesn't love me

Doubt soon begins to appear
Darkness starts to creep around
Dimmin the light along the path
Thinkin my walk to the Promise Land has stopped
He's dumbfounded as I get down on my knees to pray

Dark times don't last strong faithful people do
The world wants my light dimmed
But it gets brighter each day
Dark times don't last the word of God is forever
Believin the promises he made
Dark times will just disappear

Five Little Words

It was a just another normal day
An unexpected phone call
Sis told me you were in the hospital
I headed to the airport the next mornin
As I boarded my plane, sis called again
Tellin me that you'd already passed away

Five words weren't spoken
I didn't get to tell you goodbye
Or that I love you so much
I'm livin with the regret of not sayin
Those five little words
Those five little important words

You're up in heaven lookin down
Daddy's standin there beside you
Your spirits are beside my sister and me
Comfortin us when we're ready to cry
Sharin a smile with us in happy times
Waitin for us to join you in heaven

Five words weren't spoken
I didn't get to tell you goodbye
Or that I love you so much
I'm livin with the regret of not sayin
Those five little words
Those five little important words

Saying Goodbye

Sayin goodbye is never easy
Especially, when I'm goin home
I'll be safe in the arms of the Lord
Away from the pain and sorrow of this world
You'll feel me beside you in the darkness
When all you feel is the rain
But I don't want to say goodbye
Cause all it brings is tears

As you sit here beside me
Knowin it could be minutes or hours
When I decide to leave this earth
Left here all by yourself
Wonderin how you can go on
Lookin into our children's eyes
You're reminded of the great love we shared
But how I hate to say goodbye

Sayin goodbye is never easy
Especially, when I'm going him
I'll be safe in the arms of the Lord
Away from the pain and sorrow of this world
You'll feel me beside you in the darkness
When all you feel is rain
But I don't want to say goodbye
Cause all brings is tears

Your life will go on
You'll think of me each day
Relivin the memories we shared
Reminiscin of the good times
Holidays will be rough
Still, turn to the Lord
Believin in his promises
Knowin someday you'll be with me again

LOVE

You say you love me
That word comes easy for you
Lettin me know how much you care
Wantin for me to fall in love with you
Makin me the light of your world
Every moment away is chillin
You want me by your side
Showin me exactly how you feel

Love, it's a strong word
So heavy that it scares me
Of puttin my heart on the line
Only to get it broken
I hide it away from anyone
Who gets close enough to touch
Cause love is so life changin
I can't say it until I'm ready

Content livin my life alone

I wasn't lookin for love
Knowin how easily it falls apart
Then you stepped into my life
Lettin me see just how I could be loved
Resistin not wantin to risk my heart
I was afraid to say that four letter word
That means so much and is so precious

Have patience and believe
True love never ends, it's endurin and unchangin

Love it's a strong word
So heavy that it scares me
Of puttin my heart on the line
Only to get it broken
I hide it away from anyone
Who gets close enough to touch
Cause love is so life changin
I can't say it until I'm ready

*revised version

40

Needin Directions

Are you lost in the world
Bound by earthly things
Walkin along the same road
Goin around in circles
Not gettin no where
Wishin there was a map
Puttin you on the right path
Where you'll find the way to heaven

Are you needin directions
Leadin you out of the darkness
Breakin the devil's chains
Away from the burden and pain
Are you needin directions
To the blessed promise land
Where you'll be with the Lord
Are you needin directions

Go to any church's Sunday service
Listen to the message the pastor is preachin
He's tellin everyone of the glory
Along with the peace and salvation
We can all have, if we want it
The decision is yours to make
Is it heaven or hell
Are you ready for directions

You've now got the right directions
Leadin you to the Promise Land
Usin the Good Book as your map
Believin every word you're readin is true
Listenin to the Holy Spirit
Realizin you're a true testament
To his mercy and glory
Helpin the lost find God's love

Team Up with Jesus

Are you teamed up with the devil
Relvelin in what makes you feel good
But feelin so empty hours later
Chasin after tangible things that disappear
Are you teamed up with the devil
Livin for the ways of the world
Wantin so much to be a part of it

Team up with Jesus
Your life is gonna change

You'll never be the same
Findin purpose and passion
To really live the life you're meant to
Lovin someone other than yourself
Puttin Jesus before anything

Forget about me, myself, and I
Life can be easy instead of rough
Startin to live life for others
Blessin them with a smile
Readin the Good Book
Taught the ways to enjoy life
If you live life God's way
Learin there can be heaven on earth

Team up with Jesus
Your life is gonna change
Team up with Jesus
You'll never be the same
Findin purpose and passion
To really live the life you're meant to
Lovin someone other than yourself
Puttin Jesus first before anything

Got Jesus

Have you got Jesus
Have you got Jesus (Have you got Jesus)
Blood runnin through your veins
Lit by the eternal flame
Not worried about fortune and fame
Your life will never be the same
Have you got Jesus
Blood runnin through your veins

The world's gettin darker every day
As misery and doubt fill the air
Judgment day we can't no longer delay
Most people don't seem to care

Our lives we can't replay
So it's love we have to share
The Lord's word we need to obey
For Jesus is comin back someday
It's time to get back to the Good Book
Learnin that believin is seein
What's waitin on the other side

Is more than you and I could desire
We don't put ourselves in the fire
Cause the devil is a liar
Hearin the Lord's word our ears will never tire
We'll be the person someone will admire

Have you got Jesus
Have you got Jesus (Have you got Jesus)
Blood runnin through your veins
Lit by the eternal flame
Not worried about fortune and fame
Your life will never be the same
Have you got Jesus
Blood runnin through your veins

A New Life

Earl followed his calling to minster
Deep inside his motives weren't sincere
With help from liquor and pills
He recklessly wondered into the darkness

Day by day the light grew dimmer
His life quickly begun to slip away
Faced with death knocking at his door
Earl got down on his knees and prayed for God's help
The light of the Lord burned bright
Guidin him back onto that narrow road
Where he could see the gates of heaven
A new life for the Lord had begun

At first, the struggle seemed hard
Each day he listened to the word of God
Spent time alone readin the Bible
Still, temptations weren't far away

Earl gave his life to God
He witnesses almost every Sunday
Bein an example to non-believers
His days are spent bringin others to the Lord

A bright light burns inside of him
As he walks down that narrow road
The gates of heaven in plain view
A new life for the Lord is being lived

Who Are You With?

As the days get darker
The people get selfish and meaner
Do we live in the world ways
Do we live by the word of God
Make a choice and decide
Who are you with?

Who are you with?
The devil who strings a web of lies
Showin you deceptive illusions
Who are you with?
The Lord who can help you along the way
Givin you peace and everlasting life

The hours pass quickly, the days pass slowly
Each tick of the clock times runnin out
Darkness and meanness are closing in
We need to get faith started again
Making the world brighter
Shuttin out the darkness, so who are you with

Who are you with?
The devil who strings a web of lies
Showin you deceptive illusions
Who are you with?
The Lord who can help you along the way
Givin you peace and everlastin life

Don't Light That Fire

The devil is always around
Wantin to light embers of sin
Blowin anger and doubt
Until you burn with rage
Worried more about yourself
Concerned with how the world sees you

Don't light that fire
It will only work against you
Let the dove of peace set on your shoulder
Keepin you calm while in the flames
With patience and temperance
But don't light that fire

Circumstances will always change
But the devil wants to keep us in trouble
Stirrin up what we thought was forgotten
Still love smothers anger and fear
Let the dove set on your shoulder
Not lightin the devil's fire

Don't light that fire
It will only work against you
Let the dove of peace set on your shoulder
Keepin you calm while in the flames
With patience and temperance
But don't light that fire

Small Steps

Last year I went through a test
Losin all my friends at work
Cause of rumors and lies
I fought the good fight of faith
Until I was ready to give up
My heart wouldn't walk away
Wantin the truth to be told
Only no one would believe me

It takes small steps
Toward makin new beginnings
Learnin to take a leap of faith
Believin good fruit will grow on the vine
It takes small steps
To learn to trust again
Even though my heart is broken
It just takes small steps

For months, I asked the Lord
To let them see the truth
Wantin so much to have faith
But he begun dealing with me
I began to look at myself
Learnin that I had to change my heart
To forgive them and start over
Realizin God is testin each one of us

It takes small steps
Toward makin new beginnings
Learnin to take a leap of faith
Believin good fruit will grow on the vine
It takes small steps
To trust again
Even though my heart is broken
It just takes small steps

I Don't Have The Time

I seem to always care
What others thought of me
Always bein disappointed
By friends I assumed were friends
High expectations of equal respect
No matter what the situation
Learnin in a quiet place alone
To give my care to the Lord, so devil

I don't have the time
And I don't care
What you think of me
Cause at the end of the day
The Lord's opinion is the only one
That matters to me
I don't have the time
Oh, I don't have the time

Everyday I get ready
To do the Lord's work
Changin the life of a stranger
Showin them the love of Jesus
With encouragement and good words
Sharin a big smile
Still, there are people in the world
Expressin their dislike for me

I don't have the time
And I don't care
What you think of me
Cause at the end of the day
The Lord's opinion is the only one
That matters to me
I don't have the time
Oh, I don't have the time

What Did I Do

I get up every mornin
Show up early to work
I say hello to those who say hi
Do my job and don't complain
Thinkin of how blessed I am
Thankin the Lord for everything
By the middle of the day
I'm askin myself

What did I do
Why are people actin like that
What did I do
For them to be judgin me
What did I do
As they start laughin
What did I do
I'd sure like to know

I spend some days dumbfounded
Wonderin what the talk is
Still, I know God is in charge
I have his unchangin love
There's no need to worry
As I'm reminded of the blessings
He has gave me and will give me
Knowin everything is in his hands

What did I do
Why are people actin like that
What did I do
For them to be judgin me
What did I do
As they start laughin
What did I do
I'd sure like to know

All I have to do is live my life for him
Bein ready to feel the rain from heaven
Not worried about other people

Sunset Memories

As the sun begins to set
On the beach we stand together
Sayin vows of our love
In front of family and friends
Startin our lives together
A new chapter begins
Empty pages we'll start to write
Fillin them up with love

Sunset memories is what I'll treasure
The warm breeze of the wind
Hearin the crashin of the waves
Trustin in the word forever
The peacefulness of love
Knowin any storm we can weather
Strugglin through those moments together
Sunset memories is what I'll treasure

Life's weather won't be perfect
We'll find times to disagree
Clouds will roll in quickly

Takin the sunshine away
Powerful winds start to blow
The writin of the pages
Will be written and rewritten
Still, love is weaved inside each line

Sunset memories is what I'll treasure
The warm breeze of the wind
Hearin the crashin of the waves
Trustin in the word forever
The peacefulness of love
Knowin any storms we can weather
Strugglin through those moments together
Sunset memories is what I'll treasure

Unexpected Love

We met in the winter time at a church called harvest time
The Lord connected us usin the Bible as a tool
A strong friendship grew and before we knew it
A familiar crazy feelin , discoverin both of us had found

An unexpected love that grows deeper everyday
Filled with the Lord and complete honesty
When we're together time just slips away
An unexpected love we wouldn't trade for anything

As we start our life together on this summer day
Turin two flames into one and believin love is forever
Meanin that word that is so precious, bein patient with one another
Teachin each other about love as our journey as one begins

An unexpected love that grows deeper everyday
Filled with the Lord and complete honesty
When we're together time just slips away
An unexpected love we wouldn't trade for anything

Get Me Out of Here, Lord

Get me out of here, Lord
Take me to my heavenly home
So I can walk the streets of gold
With loved ones who've already gone home
Either livin in the city or out on the farm
My mansion in heaven isn't bought on loan
Get me out of here, Lord
Take me to my heavenly home

I spent my life working
Raised two children all alone
Teachin them God's word
The young woman has got old
Livin off the seeds I've sown
Forgettin those precious moments
My children put me in this nursin home

Get me out of here, Lord
Take me to my heavenly home
So I can walk the streets of gold

With loved ones who've already gone home
Either livin in the city or out on the farm
My mansion in heaven isn't bought on loan
Get me out here, Lord
Take me to my heavenly home

I know I'm here to stay
Wishing I could go back home
Cnas make sure I'm bathed and fed
Sometimes I get antsy wonderin how long
It will before my time on earth is though
I sit quietly waitin to hear your voice
Wantin to feel the touch of an angel
Anytime Lord you can take me home

Get me out of here, Lord
Take me to my heavenly home
So I can walk the streets of gold
With loved ones who've gone home
Either livin in the city or out on the farm
My mansion isn't bought on loan
Get me out of here, Lord
Take me to my heavenly home

Memories of Yesterday

Today I was thinkin
Celebratin Easter in Arkansas
Spendin the day out on lake
Just enjoyin each other's company
Singin "They're gonna put me in the movies"
Eatin good southern cookin
Talkin about times gone by

Memories of yesterday
I'll cherish them so much
Rememberin the good ole days
Knowin we'll meet again
Up in heaven someday
In a place where we'll never die
Relivin those precious moments
Those memories of yesterday

Time has passed quickly
Much of the family have gone home
To spend their days with the Lord
Leavin us here down on earth
Until our assignment is through
Still, I know there right beside me
Helpin me a little each day
Believin I'll see them again

Memories of yesterday
I'll cherish them so much
Rememberin the good ole days
Knowin we'll meet again
Up in heaven someday
In a place where we'll never die
Relivin those precious moments
Those memories of yesterday

The Good Life

Life was good I thought
Doing what I wanted
Never justifyin to anybody
Still, somethin was missin
I went to church one Sunday
That day I met Jesus
I turned my life over to him

The good life, oh, the good life
Livin my life for Jesus
Spendin time with him each day
Seeing the good in others
When they treat me unkindly
Helpin those in need
Feelin that heavenly rain
Right now here on earth

I find myself smilin all day
Happy with my life now
Thankful for everyone and everything
Knowin it can be taken away
Sharin my happiness with others
Encouragin people with his word
Giving every problem to the Lord

Life before Jesus was death
Now I have eternal life

The good life oh, the good life
Livin my life for Jesus
Spendin time with him each day
Seein the good in others
When they treat me unkindly
Helpin those in need
Feelin the heavenly rain
Right now here on earth

The Snake Will Bite

He'll slither in unseen
Whisperin pleasures of evil
Tellin you everything will ok
Usin examples of his power
Tearin down family and friends
Leadin you to believe they're enemies
Life becomes sad and blue
As he gets ready to strike

The snake will bite
Just when you think it's safe
Don't get too comfortable
He's coilin around you
The snake will bite
When you trust him too much
Watch out oh, watch out!
The snake will bite

Once the venom gets in
You'll do things you regret
Tellin lie after lie
People will not understand
Still, for you it's comfortable
Ruinin lives just for fun
Standin at the door thinkin it's heaven
Too late, you find out its hell

Life turns upside down fast
Find your way quickly back to Jesus

Let Jesus take out the venom
Give you peace of mind
Lookin back at your actions
Wantin to run and hide
Instead, get on your knees
Pray for forgiveness
Read his word everyday
The snake will slither away

Reality Check

At work on a warm June summer day
I went to a noonday in-service lunch
An older gentleman was the guest speaker
He talked about his experiences
That happened many years ago
Later in the day I realized
The Lord sent a message to me
It seemed to be crystal clear

It was a reality check
To be humble yet strive for greatness
A reality check for me
To be a team player

Preferrin your brother over yourself
You're blessed to be a blessin
It was a reality check

The speaker said, life is like baseball
We can't all be starters
But we all get to play the game
In the lives of people we meet
Whether it be a smile or a hello
If are our hearts are on God
His presence strongly can be felt
Showerin his love around the world

It was a reality check
To be humble yet strive for greatness
A reality check for me
To be a team player
Never knownin what God will do
Preferrin your brother over yourself
A simple yet complicated request
It was a reality check

God Is Here

There are many days
I'm not sure of myself
In this crazy world
Storms come up unexpectedly
Making me take cover
Still, I have faith
Everything is all right
As I get down on my knees

High expectations I have
In God to be there
When the clouds come up
To help me on my path
I'm not afraid of the dark
Cause I know for sure
He's with me now

The devil whispers lies
Makin me see his fiction
Instead of believing it
I tell him to get under my feet
Down there where he belongs
Cause I'm in Jesus
And he is in me

High expectations I have
In God to be there
When the clouds come up
To help me on my path
I'm not afraid of the dark
Cause I know for sure
He's with me now

Super Charged

Went to church on Wednesday night
Just to hear the word
Help recharge my batteries
Listenin to the Holy Ghost
Through me he wrote a song
Helpin another person there
To come to the father
My mind was renewed

I got super charged again
In the Holy Ghost and fire
Touched by the anointing
I got super charged again
Givin him all the glory
Thankin him for my life
I got super charged again

Oh, I got super charged again

I went to work on Thursday
Not afraid of the day
Speakin in a heavenly language
Only God would understand
Feelin he's right beside me
Feelin I'm on higher ground
And seein the latter rain

I got super charged again
In the Holy Ghost and fire
Touched by the anointin
I got super charged again
Givin him all the glory
Thankin him for my life
I got super charged again
Oh, I got super charged again

Who's Pullin Your Strings

I spend everyday
Watchin and listenin to others
Seein who runnin their lives
I'm amazed at what I see
People tryin to control people
Only to get what they want
Not caring about who they hurt
Just feelin good to put people down

Who's pullin your strings
God, the devil, or other people
Tellin you how to think
Encourage you how to feel
Who's pullin your strings

I let others be in control

Of what I thought about
And my self -worth
Put down in the darkest hole
I didn't want to come out
Then a touch from God
His hand put in control
Now, my life has changed

Who's pullin my strings, its God
Readin his word
Feeling his presence
Who's pullin my strings
The devil and other people try
My life is in God's hands
I made the change
The will of God has taken over

I Don't Have Time to Sin

I don't have time to sin
Cause I'm out spreadin God's word
You may find it absurd
But I won't be detoured
So I don't have time to sin
It's the spiritual fight I'm gonna win
So I'll tell you again
I don't have time to sin

Guided on the straight and narrow
By determined parents who believe
Learnin that God's eyes are on the sparrow
By the devil I could be deceived

Even if he may shoot a poison arrow
I will accomplish more than he can conceive
Cause he can't tempt me with being a zero
Knowing perfection I will achieve
There's a fight everyday
I turn to the word for guidance
Ask the Lord to please help me

I don't have time to sin
Cause I'm out spreadin God's word
You may find it absurd
But I won't be detoured
So I don't have time to sin
It's the spiritual fight I'm gonna win
So I'll tell you again
I don't have time to sin

It's More Than a Job

I get up every mornin
Ready to face another day
Say a little prayer
That I'm a blessin to someone
To be a light in a dark place
I do the dirty dishes hour after hour
Still, I know that my job is more
I'm there to show God's love to the patients

It's more than a job
It's a second home to me
I go to see family
It's more than a job
It's more than just about money

It's more than a job
It's a second home to me
I go there to see family

As I watch and listen
Their lookin for someone to care
Think of it more than a job
Cause it's their home
I find as I try to bless them
They sometimes end up blessing me
With just a encouraging word
Or a happy to see you smile

It's more than a job
It's a second home to me
I go to see family
It's more than a job
It's more than just about money
It's more than a job
It's a second home to me
I go there to see family

That Was Yesterday

I was makin my way to the Promise Land
When some strangers crossed my path
They took me on a slight detour
Learnin some lessons the hard way
I stopped goin to church
Begun to listen to the devil
I quickly got down on his level
I soon put the pedal to metal

With some helpful words along the way
Readin the scripture throughout the day
Help keep the negative thoughts away
Getting down on my knees to pray
I hear any word Jesus might say
Because listenin to the devil
Oh, that was yesterday

It was when I was at my lowest
God sent an angel to me
One step at a time
Admittin I was lost
Askin for a little help
Lettin Jesus back into my heart
I stepped back on the path
Confident my life is in the Lord's hands

These days Jesus is first in my life
I'm always in the pew to receive his message

With some helpful words along way
Readin the scripture throughout the day
Help keep the negative thoughts away
Gettin down on my knees to pray
I hear any word Jesus might say
Because, listenin to the devil
Oh, that was yesterday

Ghost of the Past

I do that familiar dance
Taking one step forward
Then somethin happens
I take two steps back
The light suddenly goes dark
Puttin me back in a tailspin
Walkin around in circles
Tryin to find another place to begin

Ghosts of the past
Surface every now and then
Remindin me of how far I've come
From the unconfident person I used to be
It was negative energy that followed me
the darkness is never far way
There's always that threat some might say
Ghost of the past stay a bay

People forget how they treated you
But it's somethin one never forgets
When you're yelled at or completely forgotten
As years go by, the future looks brighter
The past then makes a step into your present
Stoppin me in my tracks
Bringin thoughts of unworthiness back
My self-confidence starts to lack

Ghosts of the past
Surface every now and then
Remindin of how far I've come
From the unconfident person I used to be
It was negative energy that followed me
The darkness is never far away
There's always that threat some might say
Ghosts of the past stay at bay

Drunk on Jesus

Many people of this world like to drink
Whether it be whiskey, wine, or shots
Tryin so hard to forget their own sorrows
Wantin just to have a good time
I've tried the liquor of this world
But felt empty inside the next day
Sunday mornin at an alter I found
The kind of drink I can't get enough of

Gettin drunk on Jesus
Completely lost in the Holy Spirit
Drinkin a sweet new wine
With no hangover to worry about
Eatin up the gospel world like bread
To keep me full of his light
I want to get drunk on Jesus
I want to get drunk on Jesus

With each day I stumble a little more
Happiness is over my face
People think I'm a little bit crazy
I tell them to leave me alone
Then I remember what the Good Book says
To be kind to everyone that I meet
I say, "The water of life is so much stronger
Than anything else I could drink

Gettin drunk on Jesus
Completely lost in the Holy Spirit
Drinkin a sweet new wine
With no hangover to worry about
Eatin up the gospel word like bread
To keep me full of his light
I want to get drunk on Jesus
I want to get drunk on Jesus

Right Beside You

When we said I do it was till death do us part
That day as come too soon since God has called me home
As I leave you remember this, my love for you is forever
A flood of tears will fall but I want you to know

I'm right beside you as life quickly goes on
Right beside you when you're missin me
Wishin I was there in those sad moments
Remember me and smile cause I'm right beside you

There will be days to cry along with those to laugh
Memories are cherished as the future looks brighter
Knowin we'll see each other again at the heavenly gates
As I wait anxiously for you to be reunited again

I'm right beside you as life quickly goes on
Right beside you when you're missing me
Wishin I was there in those sad times
Remember me and smile cause I'm right beside you

Thankful for Little Things

In this world today
Children are gettin everything
From name clothes and expensive cars
Cell phones at age ten to handfuls of money
Taught everything is in reach
Throw a fit to get what they want
But what is really learned
Then parents are askin

Are you thankful
Thankful for little things
For peace and love
Friendship and kindness
Are you thankful
Thankful to the Lord
Thankful for the little things
Are you thankful

I used to be that way

Thought I was entitled to everything
Then I had a wakeup call
Things quickly begun disappearin
I need to work for lastin things
Such as self-respect and love
For family members and friends
Findin the true meanin of happiness

I'm thankful
Thankful for little things
For peace and love
Friendship and kindness
I'm thankful
Thankful to the Lord
Thankful for little things
I'm thankful for little things

A Book of Thoughts; Longing for Heaven took about eight years to write. In 2013, the lord would begin to do a work in me that I wasn't ready for. With a trial I didn't think I would recover from until I began to write down my thoughts. Those who that I needed to say to talk back to all those people who were bullying me every day. The lord taught me have my feet planted and stand tall when I found my voice to talk back and speak the truth to those people who were bullying me each day. I hope your journey through this book will help you find the courage to talk back and state the truth to those people who like to take jabs at you with their words.

A Book Of Thoughts;

Longing For Heaven

Vol. 2

Angela Tibbs

Table Of Contents

Watchin a Movie

God Connection

Put On A Cross

Are You Goin to Heaven

Spiritual High

Do You Get It

The Choice

Keep Shovlin

Kept Woman

Holdin On Tight

Bullets in the Gun

Wake Up

Watch Me

Get Over Yourself

Turned Off The Recorder

Mind Games

I'm Not Alone

Don't Want To Be Like You

No Pressure

Clean Out Your Ears

Don't Settle

Don't Be Infected

Unique Position

Don't Go Judgin Me

I'm Breakin Those Records

Turnin My Life Upside Down

Fall in the Ditch

Throwin Stones

The Best Sermon

Faith, Family, & My Guitar

It was a year ago today

People thought I'd lost my mind

The devil had come in like a flood

Finding no answers in the world

I got down on my knees and prayed

Asking God to please help me

Receivin love from my family

Playin my guitar in a quiet place

Faith, family, and my guitar

Helps me through the hard days

Faith, family, and my guitar

Gives me strength to be strong

I'd surely be lost without

Faith, family, and my guitar

Test and trials will come around

When I put the Lord first

Standin on his truthful word

The world just goes by

Spendin time with people I love

Makin a joyful noise with my guitar

Praisin god all day long

Bein a witness for him

Faith, family and my guitar

Helps me through hard days

Faith, family, and my guitar

Gives me strength to be strong

I'd surely be lost without

Faith, family, and my guitar

Gone Crazy

My emotions were running wild

I was such an unstable fool

Then someone invited me to church

That Sunday I met God

Well I gave my heart to Jesus

A new life for me had begun

As I read the good book daily

Buildin a relationship with God

They think I've gone crazy

Spendin time on my knees

They think I've gone crazy

Believin that book of old stories

They think I've gone crazy

Touched by the spirit of God

They think I've gone crazy

Cause I'm crazy for the Lord

I'm a little bit different now

Actin in a way that seems strange

Knowin Jesus is beside me each day

Gives me a positive attitude

I witness to those around me

Of God's mercy and his grace

Tellin them a story of when he

Turned this sinner into a saint

Bell Sheep

I used to be like many people

Waiting to hear the bell ring

Lettin someone else lead me

Down the path that's easy to see

It wasn't until I met Jesus

That my eyes were open wide

Now, each day I ask the Lord to

Help me lead his sheep

Let me be your bell sheep

Leadin the lost to you

Bein a light in a dark place

Showin others of your love

Let me be your bell sheep

A witness to those who don't know you

About your mercy and your grace

Let me be your bell sheep

Leadin by example

Isn't as easy as it seems

I'm bound to stumble and to fall

Teachin no one is perfect

Only Jesus is the perfect one

We all learn from one another

That miracles happen everyday

If we believe in God

Still I ask the Lord

Ground Zero

The devil hit me head on

Then surprised me from behind

Shakin my faith to the core

With doubt slowly building

Lettin my faith go to nothing

Everything begun to fall around me

I'm standin at my ground zero

Lookin up at the sky from this hole

Jesus standin at the edge lookin down

Sayin to me "Trust only in him"

I'm standin at my ground zero

Ready to rebuild my life with Jesus

As each day passes I get stronger

Spendin time in God's word

I begin to strengthen my faith

As the devil's up to his old tricks

To trip me up to fail again

But my eyes are solely on Jesus

I'm standin at my ground zero

Lookin up at the sky from this hole

Jesus standin at the edge lookin down

Sayin to me "Trust only in him"

I'm standin at my ground zero

Ready to rebuild my life with Jesus

Shut Up & Listen

All day long I hear people talkin

Thinkin they know every answer

Tryin to tell me who I am

They don't understand puttin me down

Only hurts their lives

Then they wonder why it's so bad

And I just want to say

Shut up and listen

To the Holy Ghost inside

Shut up and listen

To what God has to say

You can say your opinion

It probably won't be right

Shut up and listen

Shut up and listen

I take a moment to remember

The price Jesus paid for me

Realizin I have to love others

No matter what they may do to me

Forgivin them of their wrongs

No matter how bad they may be

In the end they'll reap what they sow

Wishin they would finally learn the lesson

Shut up and listen

To the Holy Ghost inside

Shut up and listen

To what God has to say

You can say your opinion

It probably won't be right

Shut up and listen

Shut up and listen

Up to Hell's Door

Do you live in the world?

Really live in the world

Lust, love, and money

Fallin for the devil's lie

Thinkin you're living the good life

Not worried about tomorrow

Judgin others too quickly

Runnin up to hell's door

Are you flaunting immorality?

Burnin up with jealously all day

Believin life is more fun in the dark

Walkin down the path that's big and wide

At the end of the gate where many go inside

Are you flauntin immorality?

Runnin up to hell's door

Are you runnin up to hell's door?

Many people of today

Believe their life is good

Only thinkin of what is satisfyin

Not thinkin about eternity

They're blind to the promises of God

Bein on that straight narrow path

Walkin on that wide road

Runnin up to the gates of hell

Don't Listen To The Voices

Each day I hear people say

You're not good enough

You'll never be anything

Gettin heckled over nothin

It makes me want to give up

And just sit down and cry

Still, I hear a voice say

Keep your eye upon Jesus

Don't listen to the voices

That speaks words against you

Don't listen to the voices

Who are puttin you down

Don't listen to the voices

They're only jealous of you

Listen to my voice instead

Sayin you can do anything

Spend each day in the word

Drawin closer to me

Standin on my scriptures

Knowin there is truth in them

There's a bright future ahead

Just believe in me and my father

When the days seem rough

Stand still and remember

Causin Trouble

Many times in my life I'm around

People who just want to ruin my day

Because their life isn't going right

But they don't know or realize

That I'm in the Lord

With my mind on Jesus

Trouble goes back on them

Where it started from

Tryin to cause trouble in my life

I don't receive any of it

Tryin to cause trouble in my life

You'll quickly soon find out

It goes back where it came from

I don't live with strife

Tryin to cause trouble in my life

It goes back right back to you

No matter what the devil does

The darts are reflected off

Quenched by the spirit of God

It's a waste of the devil's time

The people's time too

Cause they don't understand

Life's too short to be worrying

About trouble that isn't trouble at all

Life Lessons

With each lesson in life

I learned as I grew up in God

They seemed like stumblin blocks

I've made into steppin stones

I climbed higher with each step I took

Sometimes it was hard to learn

The trials I had to go through

Made me grow up in him

Life lessons are never easy

To go out of my comfort zone

Makin me into a better person

Into the one God wants me to be

Life lessons only get harder

It can almost break my spirit

I only seem to grow closer to him

With each life lesson

Each lesson toward freedom

But dependin on God

He walks beside me in the storm

Helpin me when I'm weak

To overcome those troubles

Maintainin a thankful spirit

Knowin I can help someone else

With the life lessons I learned

Blessingville

As I travel down life's highway

I've put roots down in many towns

Nothingville, worryville, and doubtville

Each time the devil set fire to my house

I've learned to trust the Lord

Knowinhe's right beside me

I walked out of the flames untouched

My next stop is. . .

Blessingville

A town filled with God's love

Blessingville

Where his goodness touches me

After walkin through the fire

Going to the next level of faith

Blessingville

I'm stayin in blessingville

The devil tries to take my blessins away

Puttin wrong words in my mouth

I would never ever say

Learnin to see his same tricks

I've become more aware

Puttin him under my feet

Lessons are learned each day

I'm blessed in God

Keep Talkin

You spend your day

Makin threats to hurt me

Cause I don't think like you

My faith is God is strong

And you're a non-believer

I will stand on the truth

While you're dealin with lies

In the end I'll be praisin God

Keep talkin about me

Oh, just keep talkin

And we'll surely see

Who's complainin of problems

And who's thankin God

Keepin talkin about me

Oh, just keep talkin

As you watch my life you aren't sure

I'm always happy while you're miserable

You're determined to ruin my day

Bein in the presence of the Lord

I know everything is ok

Tryin to be a livin witness to you

I quickly begin to clearly see

The devil's got you blinded from truth

Seasons

I've gone through the winter

When it was so difficult and cold

The plans I made were going no where

Ready to give up and stop believin

When tough times come along

I started to read the Lord's word

As the chilly winter begun to leave

I anticipated the comin spring

Spiritual seasons, I go through them

From the cold hash winter

To the excitin buddin of spring

The laid back feelin of summer

To the harvest time of fall

Spiritual seasons, I go through them

It's up to me how much I learn

From the seasons I go through

My heart is full and warm

I use the summer to rest

Rememberin how I helped

Family, friends, and strangers

Thankful for what God has done for me

With fall beginning to set in

Cause before the cycle can start again

The pickin of my fruit God must tend

Stop, Learn, and Listen

Walkin down a country road on Sunday afternoon

I came upon a rundown old church with a sign

It read: "Everyone's welcome in Gods house."

I walked inside where I could see

A faded weathered picture of Jesus

Lit by the through a broken window

Makin my way through the cobwebs and dust

I found a worn out Bible lyin on a pew

Standin there, I realized I needed to

Stop, and let the world go by

Learn, by readin the Bible

Listen to the Holy Ghost

Guidin me along the way

I need to stop, learn, and listen

Stop, learn, and listen

I need to stop, learn, and listen

I could see a vivid scene

Preacher preachin about hell and temptation

Adults screamin Amen and Halleluiah

Children on the edge of their seats

Bein taught the fear of God

With such raw emotion

Cuttin their teeth on Power in the Blood

And learnin how to sing

Watchin A Movie

As I walk through this life

I see it happenin to others

And it also happens to me

People judgin other people

Just because they can

Not thinkin about their future

Sometimes I want ask

Are you ready for judgment day?

Watchin a movie with God

Goin through your life story

Of how you treated others

Watchin a move with God

He's waitin for you to explain

How treatin people wrong is right

Watchin a movie with God

Are you ready for your Judgment?

We all have to take a long look

At ourselves in the mirror

Either likin or dislikin what we see

A choice as to be made

Repentin of the sins you've done

Or listenin to the devil again

Walkin down a dangerous path

I ask, are you ready for your judgment?

God Connection

I traveled in this world

On a path with no direction

Goin further into the darkness

Tempted and deceived by the devil

I looked up from a deep ditch

I saw Jesus lookin down at me

Stretchin out his hand

He said, "I'm here to save you"

I've got God connected

Supercharged by his word

The God connection

Is what I can't live without

The Holy Ghost guides me

In this darkenin world

The God connection

Is what I can't live without

He changed my life

He made me feel whole

Fillin that void inside me

As I hunger for his word

Learnin why he died for me

Buildin a strong connection

With the one who cares so much for me

I'm workin the rest of my life for Jesus

Put On A Cross

I was not born perfectly

I was born with a deformity

To society I was different from them

Too scared to ask questions to learn

They laughed and made fun of me

Many years I lived depressed

Until the day I found Jesus

Then I started to think about it

I was put on a cross

To suffer for somethin I didn't ask for

I was put on a cross

To suffer more pain and tears

So they wouldn't have to look at themselves

Findin that no one is perfect on earth

I was put on a cross

I got to know my Lord and Savior

Learnin he paid such a high price for me

Goin to the cross to be a slain lamb

His own people didn't receive him

They laughed at him at every turn

After dreamin of takin Jesus' place

I'm thankful for what he did on the cross

Taking my place at Calvary

Are You Goin To Heaven

I believe we all come from heaven

Sent here on a mission

To help each other on the path

Saving us from the world views

Rememberin our father is watching

Waitin for us to call on him

Livin the right way to be an example

Showin them life can be good

Are you goin to heaven

Are you goin to hell

Walkin with God each day

Or doin what you want

The choice is yours

Are you goin to heaven

Or the place of fire

Many people think I'm crazy

To believe in a fairytale

That is what they believe

But at the end of the day

I want to say to them

Who's the happier one

The one who believes in God

Or you thinkin the world is best

Spiritual High

I've heard people say

Man, I want to get high

To escape my troubles

Thinkin only earthly ways

Can take them to that place

Then I tell them of my God

And of the Holy Spirit

Get on a spiritual high

In the presence of God

It's so much better than

Weed, heroin, and cocaine

Get on a spiritual high

Lost in the Holy Spirit

You can get so high

You don't have to come down

Earthly things leave a void

But God will never leave

Speakin in a heavenly language

Lost in the presence of God

Troubles slowly go away

And everything is ok

Knowin he walks beside me

I can praise him anytime

It takes readin and mediatin on God's word

To truly be on a spiritual high

Do You Get IT

As I walk through life

I meet many people who believe

In God's and his word

But when problems arise

I hear them say "If it's God's will"

Believin he let it happen

I get so frustrated at times

And I just want to say

Do you get it?

Do you really get it?

Jesus died for us

Took our infirmity's away

What he did at Calvary

Do you get it?

Do you really get it?

He healed us from everything

I was a doubter too

Believin in the Bible

But was really not convinced

Until the day Jesus healed me

From completely losing my mind

Cause of what the devil was doing

I finally got a hold of it one day

I have victory in Jesus

The Choice

One night I had a dream

My family and I were standing in line

At those pearly gates of heaven

As we started to walk inside

I was quickly stopped and told

Just your family can go inside

I woke up in a cold sweat

Realizin to make it to heaven

I have to make a choice

To surrender my life to God

Washed clean by the blood of Jesus

I have to make a choice

To be a witness for the Lord

Showin every one of his mercy

I have to make a choice

I have to make a choice

I remember it very well

When my life went haywire

I was barely seventeen

My parents had gotten divorced

By December mom was married again

Feelin so much anger and so alone

I fell deeper into resentment

Totally filled with unforgiveness

I took drugs of this world

To escape the reality around me

(Cont)

Beln led by the devil into darkness

Walkin away from everything I loved

Livin on the street with nothing

I was ready to end my life

When an angel was sent to me

Tellin me I had a choice to make

I have to make a choice

To surrender my life to God

Washed clean by the blood of Jesus

I have to make a choice

To be a witness for the Lord

Showin every one of his mercy

I have to make a choice

I have to make a choice

Keep Shovlin

You spend your day

Makin up lies about me

Just to ruin my day

But you don't realize

I know the savior

Where I'm in perfect peace

Knowin where 'I'm bound

When judgment day comes

Keep shovlin that dirt

Heap it up nice and tall

Cause it's all your trouble

You're tryin to put on me

Keep shovlin that dirt

Complain of how bad your life is

Keep shovlin that dirt

Open your eyes and look

At the mountain of trouble

That's right in front of you

Keep shovlin that dirt

Heap it up nice and tall

Cause it's all your trouble

You're tryin to put on me

Keep shovlin that dirt

Complain how bad your life is

Keep shovlin that dirt

Kept Woman

Years ago I gave my life to Jesus

Gettin out of Egypt

Headed for the promise land

After reading God's word

My life completely change

Believin God keeps his promises

I stepped into abundance

As I lived my life for him

I'm a kept woman

God takes care of me

I'm a kept woman

He takes care of everything

I'm a kept woman

No worries or concerns

I'm a kept woman

God takes care of me

I'm Holdin On Tight

Life sometimes seems like

A bull ride in a rodeo

Trouble arrives to knock me off

I've got to deal with it

As I'm goin around in circles

Tryin to stay in the middle

I keep my eye on Jesus

Havin just a little faith

The devil opens the gate

I'm turnin round and round

Holdin tight to God's promises

Not doubtin his word

I'm holdin on tight

Stayin on for eight seconds

To hear the buzzer go off

Beatin the devil's trouble

If I end up in the dirt

Cause I'm in doubt

Lettin the devil think he's won

I'll stand right back up

Gettin back on the bull again

More determined to stand on the truth

Overcomin the obstacles

And to always be victorious

46

Bullets in the Gun

Every day that old devil

Fires deadly darts at me

To hit my weak spots

Gettin me to the ground

But I turn to the Bible

Soakin in God's word

I'm not goin to live in fear

Gettin my gun out I open the chamber

Puttin the bullets in the gun

One filled with Holy Ghost

One filled with God's word

47

The last one filled with power

Puttin bullets in the gun

Gettin ready to fight

Puttin the bullets in the gun

Ready to shoot

Aimin the gun at him

A take a firm stance

Firin it straight at him

One bullet at a time

Knockin him to his feet

So he better just run

Bein so deep in God

The devil is powerless

Wake Up

The devil controls this world

It's in such an uproar

Filled with such strife

People thinkin they're better

Than people around them

Alcohol and drug he uses

To keep you away from

The presence of the Lord

Wake up! Wake up!

I'm tellin you to wake up

The time is quickly comin

For Jesus to come down here

Wake up! Wake up!

Are you goin to go up

At the time of the rapture

Wake up! Wake up!

Instead of livin in the world's way

Give your life to Jesus

Lookin toward goin to heaven

This world gets dimmer

Findin such immeasurable peace

And a very sound mind

Ready to take a ride to the sky

When the angel sounds the trumpet

Watch Me

I spend each day of work

Hearin people laugh at me

Cause I'm chasin after my dreams

Livin my life God's way

Doin what he tells me to do

Bein a livin witness to him

Tellin everyone of his miracles

I'll have to say to them is

Watch me!

Prove you wrong

Watch me!

Do what's in my heart

Fulfillin God's purpose for my life

Seein my dreams come true

Watch me!

Do the impossible before your eyes

My dreams maybe too high for you

And you don't believe in me

I'm goin to turn them into reality

Watch me!

Prove you wrong

Watch me!

Do what's in my heart

Fulfillin God's purpose for my life

Seein my dreams come true

Watch me

Do the impossible before your eyes

Get Over Yourself

That time when everything was right

That time when you were so good

It wasn't just all you

Helpin you shine that light

It wasn't you when things fell into place

In your mind I'm sure it was

It's wasn't just all you

It was all God

Get over yourself

Thinkin you're the best

You did it all by yourself

There's someone helpin you

Get over yourself

Don't ignore him when he talks

God's got something important to say

So get over yourself

Take time to be grateful

For what he's done for you

He's the reason you're so blessed

Get over yourself

Thinkin you're the best

You did it all by yourself

There's someone helpin you

Get over yourself

Don't ignore him when he talks

God's got somethin important to say

So get over yourself

Shut off the Tape Recorder

Every day I go to work

Listenin to people talk about me

How I'm not good enough

Then the tape recorder clicks

The tape records what's said

Repeatin itself over and over again

Gettin deeper into my spirit

But I finally took control

I shut off the tape recorder

I'm not listenin to it anymore

Not lettin the devil win

I shut off the tape recorder

I'm worth somethin to God

Standin on his word

Fillin up with the Holy Ghost

I shut off the tape recorder

I'm replacin your garbage

With the truth of God

Knowin he will deliver me

I shut off the tape recorder

I'm not listenin to it anymore

Not letting the devil win

I shut off the tape recorder

I'm worth somethin to God

Standin on his word

Fillin up with the Holy Ghost

I shut off the tape recorder

56

Mind Games

I thought that givin life to Jesus

My life would get easier

I was so, so, so wrong

I began the battle of my life

Fightin the good fight of faith

Learnin to lean on God

To have a sound mind

The devil playin mind games

Tryin to psych me out

To get me away from God

Tellin me I'm not good enough

The devil's playin mind games

To trick me out of my salvation

Tryin to keep me away from the Lord

It takes mediatin on the word

Both day and night

Fully persuaded to believe

God is right beside me

When I'm tested and tried

Showin me the truth

In the mist of the fire

Wisdom in the word outsmarts the devil

I'm Not Alone

I'm not alone

As I walk through each day

I'm not alone

When trouble comes my way

God is beside me

Makin a way to walk through

Puttin my faith in him

I'm never by myself

It's stayin in the word

And so close to god

Feelin I'm in his presence

When I really don't

Knowin he's workin all the time

As nothin seems to change

Believin angels are around me

Praisin him all day long

When the devil comes at me

I tell him he better just run

I'm deeply rooted in God

Ready to stand and fight

I'm not alone

As I walk through each day

I'm not alone

When trouble comes my way

God is beside me

Don't Want To Be Like You

As I watch those around me

I've noticed one thing

Concerned about bein heard

Along with being seen

Thinkin they know everything

Always voicin their opinions

When they should be quiet

Not seein the mountain they're buildin

I don't want to be like you

I don't want to be like you

Hateful, jealous, and ignorant

You miss the Lord's touch

Deaf to hear him call your name

I don't want to be like you

I don't want to be like you

They're opinion isn't important

I don't care about what they say

I've got a news flash for them

They made a choice to be against me

So I made the choice to walk away

I want to just tell them

The mountain you're buildin

Is going to be hard for you to climb

No Pressure

I recently went through a trial

Being tested and tried

Accused of somethin I will never be

From people who just want to bother me

Showin their own stupidity

Tryin to build pressure around me

But God gave me the key

No pressure

I've got no pressure on me

As long as I know

I'm right with my God

No pressure

I've got no pressure on me

To even worry about false accusations

I've got no pressure on me

The answer wasn't easy to see

I had to go down in the valley

Until God revealed it to me

It doesn't matter what they say

I'm livin for my savior

Talkin to him each day

Bein faithful and praising him

The troubles will go away

Clean Out Your Ears

I went through a trial

Where a misunderstandin occurred

People calling me somethin I would never be

And a life I don't believe in

The devil had a stronghold on me

But those chains were broken

By keepin my eyes on Jesus

Clean out your ears

So you can hear clear

Clean out your ears

In case God comes near

Clean out your ears

If he wants to speak to you

And whisper the truth in your ear

I've talked until I'm blue in the face

But they think it's funny

To be their daily clown

And amusement for the day

I got somethin important to say

That my life isn't what you believe

Watch how I live my life each day

In the presence of the Lord

Don't Settle

There are people in this world

Who settle for almost nothin

Lettin others tell them how high to fly

And what goals they can reach

I used to be one of those people

Lettin people tell me what to dream

Don't settle for less than Gods best

Don't settle for what people think

Don't settle until you reach your goal

Don't settle for less than Gods best

Don't settle for less than Gods best

Oh, don't settle for anything less

I see past these four walls around me

Straight up toward the stars

Everyday chasin after the dreams

God put in my heart at a young age

From bein on a stage to buyin a new Cadillac

I'm not settlin for what people tell me to

I'm not settlin for less than Gods best

I'm not settlin for what people think

I'm not settlin until I reach my goals

I'm not settlin for less than Gods best

I'm not settlin for less than Gods best

I'm not settlin for anything less

Don't Be Infected

As we walk in this world

We're surrounded by negativity

People who want to cause pain

And make us cry many tears

Unaware of what's goin on

We'll start actin like someone else

Not knowin how our life will change

By what we accept in our life

Don't be infected by the devil

Be the influence

Showin people kindness and love

Don't be infected by the devil

By the bitterness of people

Be the influence showin mercy

Changin the hearts around you

Don't be infected by the devil

I used to be one of those people

Affected by it in many ways

From depression to anger

I made a choice about my future

Whether to be happy full of joy

(cont)

71

Influencin those around me

Or consumed by bad feelings

And infected those around me

I'm not bein infected by the devil

I'm goin to be the influence

Showin people kindness and love

Not bein infected by the devil

Or the bitterness people hold on to

I'm showin people mercy

Changin hearts around me

I'm not bein infected by the devil

Unique Position

Back in the summer time

The devil tried to ruin my life

Talkin through my mouth

About a life I don't believe in

Cause I live my life for God

Standin on the holy word

I was delivered out of the fire

And months later I found that

God put me in a unique position

To spread the gospel word

To open ears and eyes

I'm in a unique position

To help change lives sharing the gospel word

To bring souls to him

Don't Go Judgin Me

People today are in a rush

To judge others by the way they look

Or by the mistakes they make

Closing their ears off to the truth

That is said to them

Or actions that are plain to see

They need to open their ears

Open their eyes to the truth

Don't go judgin me

Until you watch how I live

Don't go judgin me

Until you see who comes first

I live for God everyday

Makin sure people see

That without him I'm nothin

Take a moment to realize

With just a flip of the coin

It could be you they're talkin about

Don't go judgin me

Until you watch how I live

Don't go judgin me

Until you see who comes first

I live for God everyday

Makin sure people see

That without him I'm nothin

I'm Breakin Those Records

Everyday you keep trying

To destroy me and my life

With lies about me

I listened to them for awhile

Lettin your music get me

To where I didn't want to live

But Jesus found me there

Pullin me out the devil's fire

Devil you need to go away

I'm not listenin to your lies

I'm breakin those records

Right over your head

Into a thousand pieces

I'm breakin those records

Right over your head

Givin them back to you

I replaced it with God's word

Listenin to new songs

I can do all things through Christ

God is always with me

Angels are beside me

And I'm covered by the blood

I'm in the place of peace

So I'm going to yell and say

Turnin Your life Upside Down

I've been going through a trial

Where the devil has closed ears

So that the truth couldn't be heard

Still, I stood on God's word

Knowin his promises he keeps

Until I cracked the devil's hold

Speakin the holy word

He's turnin my life upside down

Takin my life to a new level

Where a rush of overflow

Begun to soak my spirit

He's turnin my life upside down

To show others how real he is

To be a livin witness for him

Its knowin my life is God's

I trust he's beside me

Makin a way for me

Before I put my foot down

Shakin me up each day

With the help of the Holy Ghost

To make me a better witness

Tellin people of his goodness

Fall in the Ditch

I'm dealin with people

Who think they're right about me

But it's a record I want to break

Cause it's nothin but a lie

Chains that have been broken

With words of truth

Some days I want to say

Fall in the ditch

Go ahead you need to

Just fall in the ditch

So you can look up and see

Jesus sayin "I'm here to help you"

80

Makin a choice to finally

Turn from your wicked ways

When you fall you've got to look up

At the only who can save you

But you have a choice to make

Fall in the ditch

Go ahead you need to

Just fall in the ditch

So you can look up and see

Jesus sayin "I'm here to help you"

Makin a choice to finally

Turn from your wicked ways

Don't Go Throwin Stones

I go to work everyday

Dealin with the same people

Their tryin to ruin me

By the lie that's nasty

Thinkin it will kill me

But I've got news for them

I'm deeply rooted in God

That lie will just fall off of me

Don't go throwin stones at me

When they're nothin but a lie

Just to build your ego up

Don't go throwin stones at me

You have to take a minute and think

Stones you're throwin will someday

Be thrown back at you in the same manner

Don't go throwin stones at me

I've got five stones in my bag

The stone of truth

Rightness and the Holy Ghost

The livin word and strength

But I only need one stone

To stop the lies you're tellin

The truth is all I need

To stop your stone throwin

The Best Sermon

When I was lost in the world

I didn't really understand how

My life affects those around me

In many different ways

It wasn't until I got saved

God showed me a picture

Of what my life should be

To strive to be like Jesus

The best sermon is my life

It's how I live each day

To show the world God is real

The best sermon is my life

Being about my father's business

To help the lost find Jesus

The best sermon is my life

Yes, it's my life

Sharin God's word

Such a change can be made

To bring the lost into the kingdom

Showin the power and the anointin

But I know it's going to take

The livin proof of my own story

To change the minds of unbelievers

To see the truth and the light

Order Form

Bell Sheep Publishing

214 E. 10th Street

Georgetown, Illinois   61846

(217) 474-0410

Bonnie, Dexter, & Jesus

Paperback book...........................$8.28____qty

Small Town Dreams; Beginnings

Paperback book...........................$8.28____qty

Hardcover book...........................$17.28___qty

Small Town Dreams; The Lives Of Teenagers

Paperback book……………………………….$8.28___qty

Hardcover book……………………………….$17.28__qty

Bonnie, Dexter, & Jesus; Hearing The Call Of The Lord

Paperback…………………………………..$8.28___qty

A Book Of Thoughts; Longing For Heaven

 Paperback…………………………………..$8.28___qty

 Shipping

 1-10 books……………………….$5.28

 10-20…………………………..$9.28

 20 or more……………………..$15.28

 Qty_____

 Subtotal_____

 Shipping_____

 Total_____